S

R

Maverick
Early Readers

'Sniffer Dog' and 'Robber Ron'
An original concept by Katie Dale
© Katie Dale

Illustrated by Letizia Rizzo

Published by MAVERICK ARTS PUBLISHING LTD
Studio 11, City Business Centre, 6 Brighton Road,
Horsham, West Sussex, RH13 5BB
© Maverick Arts Publishing Limited November 2019
+44 (0)1403 256941

ISBN 978-1-84886-623-2

www.maverickbooks.co.uk

This book is rated as: Pink Band (Guided Reading)
This story is decodable at Letters and Sounds Phase 2.

Sniffer Dog

and

Robber Ron

By Katie Dale

Illustrated by Letizia Rizzo

The Letter S

Trace the lower and upper case letter with a finger. Sound out the letter.

Around,
around

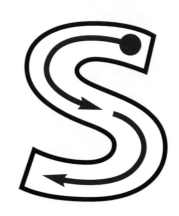

Around,
around

Some words to familiarise:

sniff   bag   snack

High-frequency words:

a

Tips for Reading 'Sniffer Dog'

- Practise the words listed above before reading the story.

- If the reader struggles with any of the other words, ask them to look for sounds they know in the word. Encourage them to sound out the words and help them read the words if necessary.

- After reading the story, ask the reader what Pip's job is.

Fun Activity

Discuss what Pip's next mission could be.

Sniffer Dog

MISSING

Sniff, sniff, sniff!

Pip smells a cat.

Ruff, ruff!

Sniff, sniff, sniff!

Pip smells a bag.

Sniff, sniff, sniff!

Pip smells a robber!

Sniff, sniff, sniff!

Pip smells a snack!

Ruff, ruff, ruff!

The Letter R

Trace the lower and upper case letter with a finger. Sound out the letter.

Down,
up,
around

Down,
up,
around,
down

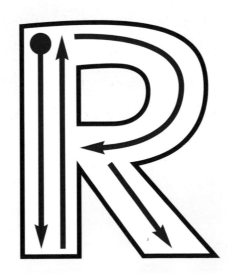

Some words to familiarise:

Robber   hat   van

High-frequency words:

a

Tips for Reading 'Robber Ron'

- *Practise the words listed above before reading the story.*
- *If the reader struggles with any of the other words, ask them to look for sounds they know in the word. Encourage them to sound out the words and help them read the words if necessary.*
- *After reading the story, ask the reader why Ron dressed as a robber.*

Fun Activity

Design a party costume!

Robber Ron

Robber Ron gets a hat.

Robber Ron gets a mask.

Robber Ron gets a sack.

Robber Ron gets a van.

Robber Ron gets a shock!

Robber Ron gets a hug.

Book Bands for Guided Reading

The Institute of Education book banding system is a scale of colours that reflects the various levels of reading difficulty. The bands are assigned by taking into account the content, the language style, the layout and phonics. Word, phrase and sentence level work is also taken into consideration.

Maverick Early Readers are a bright, attractive range of books covering the pink to white bands. All of these books have been book banded for guided reading to the industry standard and edited by a leading educational consultant.

Pink

Red

Yellow

Blue

Green

Orange

Turquoise

Purple

Gold

White

To view the whole Maverick Readers scheme, visit our website at
www.maverickearlyreaders.com

Or scan the QR code above to view our scheme instantly!